LSU TIGERS

BY
TESSA MILLER

INSIDE COLLEGE FOOTBALL

MEDIA ENHANCED BOOKS
AV² BY WEIGL
ADDED VALUE • AUDIO VISUAL

www.av2books.com

Go to **www.av2books.com**, and enter this book's unique code.

BOOK CODE

AVP38854

AV² by Weigl brings you media enhanced books that support active learning.

AV² provides enriched content that supplements and complements this book. Weigl's AV² books strive to create inspired learning and engage young minds in a total learning experience.

Your AV² Media Enhanced books come alive with...

Audio
Listen to sections of the book read aloud.

Video
Watch informative video clips.

Embedded Weblinks
Gain additional information for research.

Try This!
Complete activities and hands-on experiments.

Key Words
Study vocabulary, and complete a matching word activity.

Quizzes
Test your knowledge.

Slideshow
View images and captions, and prepare a presentation.

... and much, much more!

Published by AV² by Weigl
350 5th Avenue, 59th Floor
New York, NY 10118
Website: www.av2books.com

Library of Congress Control Number: 2018968216

ISBN 978-1-7911-0117-6 (hardcover)
ISBN 978-1-7911-0118-3 (multi-user eBook)
ISBN 978-1-7911-0119-0 (single-user eBook)

Printed in Guangzhou, China
1 2 3 4 5 6 7 8 9 0 23 22 21 20 19

042019
102318

Project Coordinator: Jared Siemens   Designer: Terry Paulhus

Every reasonable effort has been made to trace ownership and to obtain permission to reprint copyright material. The publishers would be pleased to have any errors or omissions brought to their attention so that they may be corrected in subsequent printings.

The publisher acknowledges Alamy, Getty Images, Newscom, and Wikimedia Commons as its primary image suppliers for this title.

INSIDE COLLEGE FOOTBALL

LSU Tigers

CONTENTS

Introduction

Louisiana State University (LSU) is located in Baton Rouge, Louisiana. The university was founded in 1853. It is considered the first official university of Louisiana. The campus boasts more than 250 buildings. It sits on the banks of the Mississippi River. In 2017, more than 30,000 students were enrolled in its undergraduate and graduate programs.

LSU's football team played its first game on November 25, 1893. The team's first win came in 1894 when it beat Natchez Athletic Club 26–0. Since then, the LSU Tigers have built a powerful football program. Currently, there are 117 players on the team's **roster**. In its history, LSU has belonged to three different conferences in the National Collegiate Athletic Association (NCAA). The team is now part of the Southeastern Conference (SEC). LSU has a history of winning. It also has one of the most loyal fan bases in college football.

Junior linebacker Devin White has been a permanent team captain for the Tigers since 2017. White is considered one of LSU's best players of all time.

Wide receiver Jonathan Giles wore LSU's number 7 jersey for a few games during the 2018 season because of his excellent performance at the team's preseason practices. The number 7 is worn by LSU's best playmakers, and is typically not a player's permanent number.

LSU

LOUISIANA STATE UNIVERSITY

Stadium Tiger Stadium

Division Southeastern Conference (SEC) Western

Head Coach Ed Orgeron

Location Baton Rouge, Louisiana

National Championships 3

Nicknames Fighting Tigers, Bayou Bengals, LSU

33 Head Coaches

50 Bowl Game Appearances

15 Conference Championships

35 All-American Players

History

The **highest-scoring game** in LSU history was 93–0 against the Southwestern Louisiana Institute of Liberal and Technical Learning in 1936.

LSU halfback Billy Cannon threw the pass that led to the only touchdown of the 1959 Sugar Bowl. The LSU Tigers defeated the Clemson Tigers 7–0, and Cannon was named the game's MVP.

Since its first game in 1893, LSU football has grown into a successful program. In its early years, LSU competed as an independent team and did not join a conference until 1922. During that time, it was part of the Southern Intercollegiate Athletic Association, which did not set limits on which teams could play each other. This freed the team to be able to play anyone it wanted. In 1922, LSU joined the Southern Conference to compete against other conference teams for conference and national titles.

The Tigers football team has played every year since it began, except for one. World War I (1914–1918) prevented many colleges from having football teams in 1918. This was due to the fact that men and boys were needed in the U.S. Armed Forces. Some colleges, including LSU, canceled their football programs. LSU has played more than 1,200 games in its history. It has a winning percentage of .625, with more than 750 wins, about 400 losses, and about 50 ties. This makes it one of the strongest teams in the SEC and in the entire NCAA.

LSU's first game in 1893 ended in a loss to Tulane University, which launched a long-standing rivalry between the two teams. The Tigers' first coach, Dr. Charles Coates, bought purple and gold ribbons for the players to wear on their uniforms during the game, and the colors became the official colors of LSU.

The Stadium

After the Louisiana State University band's famous pregame show, where it performs "Pregame Salute" and "Touchdown for LSU," the band forms a tunnel in the north end zone for the players to run through as they enter the field.

Since 1924, the LSU Tigers football team has played in Tiger Stadium. Originally, the stadium held 12,000 fans. After many **renovations** over the years, the stadium now holds more than 100,000 fans. In 2014, the stadium set an attendance record of 102,321 fans. It is the third-largest stadium in the SEC, the sixth-largest in the NCAA, and the seventh-largest stadium in the world.

Many people refer to the stadium by its nickname, "Death Valley." A survey conducted by the College Football Association in 1987 listed Tiger Stadium as the most difficult stadium to play in for an opposing team. It is incredibly challenging for opponents because of the noise and intensity of the LSU fans. Many players say it is like playing inside a drum. A play in the last seconds of a game in 1988 created so much fan noise and excitement that the reaction registered as a real earthquake on the university's **seismograph** equipment. The Tigers have won more than 350 games in their home stadium.

LSU's large LED end zone scoreboards are turned on every night from 6 PM to 6 AM, seven days a week, even when there are no football games or events in the stadium. University officials cite the thick Baton Rouge humidity as the reason, stating that the lights help burn off moisture buildup that could damage the screens.

Where They Play

Welcome to Tiger Stadium, home of the Louisiana State University Tigers. Loyal Tigers fans gather to watch the their team dominate on the field, filling the seats with purple and gold. The dance team and spirit squad perform as the marching band plays and the crowd cheers. Death Valley is ready for another opponent.

SEC WEST

1. **Auburn University**
   Auburn, Alabama
2. ★ **Louisiana State University**
   Baton Rouge, Louisiana
3. **Mississippi State University**
   Starkville, Mississippi
4. **Texas A&M University**
   College Station, Texas
5. **University of Alabama**
   Tuscaloosa, Alabama
6. **University of Arkansas**
   Fayetteville, Arkansas
7. **University of Mississippi**
   Oxford, Mississippi

Arena
Tiger Stadium

Location
Baton Rouge, Louisiana

Broke Ground
1924

Completed
November 25, 1924

Surface
Real Grass

Features

- Sixth-largest stadium in the United States
- The stadium's offices were once dorms where about 1,500 LSU students lived
- The New Orleans Saints played four games at Tiger Stadium in 2005 when they were displaced by Hurricane Katrina

SEC EAST

1. **University of Florida**
   Gainesville, Florida
2. **University of Georgia**
   Athens, Georgia
3. **University of Kentucky**
   Lexington, Kentucky
4. **University of Missouri**
   Columbia, Missouri
5. **University of South Carolina**
   Columbia, South Carolina
6. **University of Tennessee**
   Knoxville, Tennessee
7. **Vanderbilt University**
   Nashville, Tennessee

NORTH DAKOTA
SOUTH DAKOTA
MINNESOTA
WISCONSIN
MICHIGAN
NEW YORK
NEW HAMPSHIRE
VERMONT
MAINE
MASSACHUSETTS
RHODE ISLAND
CONNECTICUT
NEW JERSEY
DELAWARE
MARYLAND
WASHINGTON, D.C.
PENNSYLVANIA
NEBRASKA
IOWA
ILLINOIS
INDIANA
OHIO
WEST VIRGINIA
VIRGINIA
KANSAS
MISSOURI
KENTUCKY
NORTH CAROLINA
TENNESSEE
SOUTH CAROLINA
OKLAHOMA
ARKANSAS
MISSISSIPPI
ALABAMA
GEORGIA
TEXAS
LOUISIANA
FLORIDA
Atlantic Ocean
Gulf of Mexico
1
2
3
4
5
6
7
1
2
3
4
5
6
7
SCALE
0 miles
500 miles
0 kilometers
500 km
LEGEND
Home Stadium
SEC West
SEC East
United States
Other Countries
Water

The Uniforms

In 2014, the **tiger head** graphic on LSU's helmets was updated to look more threatening.

Every LSU jersey is worn with gold pants. This has been the team's preference for 50 years.

LSU's colors have been purple and gold since the first team took the field over 120 years a ago. The Tigers' traditional jerseys have been white with gold and purple shoulder stripes since 1857. LSU sometimes wears purple alternate home jerseys. Most teams have separate home and away jerseys, but the Tigers are unique. They get to wear white for both home games and away games. In 1995, Head Coach Gerry DiNardo lobbied the NCAA to allow the Tigers to wear white jerseys all the time. He won. The Tigers are the only team in the NCAA that are allowed this special right.

However, there have been some minor jersey changes. The biggest, most recent change to LSU's traditional white jerseys was a slight reduction of the shoulder stripes, which previously extended all the way to the edge of the sleeves. The helmet is bright yellow with a white stripe and two purple stripes down the center. Each side is adorned with a tiger head, along with the school's initials.

The Tigers' 2018 alternate uniform paid tribute to the team's 1918 "Silent Season," when many LSU players were fighting in World War I instead of playing football. The helmets featured a 1918 U.S. flag decal and an iridescent finish that made them look like Mardi Gras beads.

Student Athletes

LSU's graduation success rate for student athletes was **90 percent** in 2017, an all-time high for the university.

Tigers quarterback Joe Burrow transferred to LSU for his final two years of eligibility after graduating from Ohio State University as an Academic All-Big Ten and a Scholar-Athlete.

Being a college student athlete is hard work. Student athletes have to perform well on the football field and in the classroom. LSU student athletes are required to maintain a 2.3 grade point average (GPA) or higher in their core classes. They must also be registered as full-time students. LSU student athletes have access to academic mentoring and a tutorial program. LSU offers many other services to help students balance the academic and athletic life.

Many student athletes are given athletic scholarships. An athletic scholarship is a financial aid agreement between athletes and their college. Athletes who do not receive an athletic scholarship can also be "walk-on" members of the team. This means they are on the team, but without athletic financial aid. LSU typically awards the maximum number of football scholarships allowed, which is 85. LSU also awards cost of attendance scholarships to help cover costs for basic needs, such as clothing and trips home.

Cox Communications Academic Center for Student-Athletes provides football players and other LSU athletes with technology, tutoring support, and career preparation to ensure their success off the field.

Bowl Games

LSU has played in 19-straight bowl games since 2000, the **second-longest** bowl game streak in the SEC and fourth-longest in the NCAA.

In 2016, the Tigers defeated the University of Louisville Cardinals 29–9 in their first Citrus Bowl in team history. The Tigers returned to the Citrus Bowl the following season, but were defeated by the Fighting Irish of the University of Notre Dame.

Bowl games are a unique sports tradition in college football. In the beginning of college football, there was no true **postseason**. Today, a variety of postseason bowl games are played. Bowl games give teams the opportunity to continue striving for recognition and victory after the end of regular play. There are currently 40 bowl games played in various combinations each year. These games are chosen with input from teams, sponsors, and the College Football Playoff Selection Committee. The game **matchups** are announced in December.

LSU has played in 50 bowl games. They have won 26, lost 23, and tied 1. LSU has played in the Sugar Bowl the most, with 13 games. The Sugar Bowl is played each year in New Orleans and has been played since 1935. It is considered one of the most important bowl games for southern universities.

LSU defeated Notre Dame 41–14 in the 2007 Sugar Bowl. The game marked the Sugar Bowl's return to New Orleans, after being played in the Georgia Dome the previous year due to Hurricane Katrina.

The Coaches

Dr. Charles E. Coates was the first coach at LSU. He only coached one game, the first game, and lost.

After being named interim head coach just a few games into the 2016 season, Ed Orgeron made immediate changes to the team's style of play and coaching staff. Orgeron was named the permanent head coach on November 26, 2016, and under his leadership, the Tigers finished the season 6–2.

For many LSU fans, it is difficult to pick the team's top coaches. Only eight coaches have stayed with LSU for five or more seasons, and only seven have won a conference title. However, the Tigers have had many successes under their 33 head coaches. Ed Orgeron has been the head coach since 2016. He followed Les Miles, who many claim was LSU's best coach in the team's history.

PAUL DIETZEL Paul Dietzel coached from 1955 to 1961. Dietzel is famous for his use of the "three-platoon system." He replaced entire groups of players to maintain energy on the field throughout the game. Dietzel's system led the Tigers to their first National Championship in 1958. Dietzel is the only LSU coach to have a perfect season since 1908.

CHARLES MCCLENDON Charles McClendon was LSU's longest-serving coach. In his 18-year career with LSU, from 1962 to 1979, he only had one losing season. He has the most wins for any coach in LSU history, with 137. McClendon is one of the most revered coaches in LSU football. His fans affectionately called him "Cholly Mac."

LES MILES Les Miles is considered LSU's most successful coach. He led the team to two SEC titles. He has also had the winningest record in LSU history. He led the team to 10-game winning seasons six times. He was the second coach to have a 13-game winning season. Miles coached from 2005 to 2016.

The Mascot

After accompanying the cheerleaders onto the field at Tiger Stadium, Mike the Tiger's cage was parked near the opponent's locker room at the end of the stadium, so the other team would have to walk past him on their way onto the field.

Mike the Tiger is the official mascot of LSU. He is a live Bengal-mix tiger that lives on campus. The current Mike was born on September 13, 2016. He is the seventh "Mike" in LSU history. He was brought to LSU in 2017. All of the Mikes have lived in a **habitat** on LSU's campus. Mike even has his own Facebook page and website.

Up until the end of the 2016 season, Mike rode into Tiger Stadium in a special cage on wheels. That stopped when the sixth Mike refused to enter the cage. Now Mike stays in his habitat and a costumed Mike the Mascot takes the field for games.

The costumed Mike the Mascot made his first appearance at LSU in the 1980s. He does **stunts** with the spirit squad and dances on the sidelines during games. Students who play Mike are considered athletes at LSU. They receive a partial scholarship, compete in cheerleading competitions, and must maintain a certain GPA.

In 2015, Mike the Mascot showed off his dance moves in a music video with country singer Brad Paisley.

Legends of the Past

For many players, their time with the Tigers is the start of a promising football career. These are some of the best-known football players to play for Louisiana State.

Patrick Peterson

Patrick Peterson played for LSU from 2008 to 2010. He came into the program as one of the most **decorated** high school players in LSU history. In 2010, Peterson won the Chuck Bednarik Award, which is the highest award for a defensive player. Peterson also won the Jim Thorpe Award for best defensive back in college football. In 2011, the Arizona Cardinals **drafted** Peterson in the first round of the National Football League (NFL) draft. He was the first cornerback chosen. In his 125 games with the Cardinals, Peterson has had 380 tackles and 23 career interceptions.

Position: Cornerback
Seasons: 2008–2010 (LSU Tigers), 2011–Present (Arizona Cardinals)
Born: July 11, 1990, Pompano Beach, Florida

Leonard Fournette III

Leonard Fournette III was a running back for LSU from 2014 to 2016. He saw his most successful year with LSU during the 2015 season. That season, Fournette broke multiple school records. With 1,953 rushing yards and 22 rushing touchdowns in a single season, many experts regarded him as the greatest player in college football. In 2017, he was a first-round draft pick by the Jacksonville Jaguars. The team finished the season 10–6, with Fournette providing key support in his position.

Position: Running Back
Seasons: 2014–2016 (LSU Tigers), 2017–Present (Jacksonville Jaguars)
Born: January 18, 1995, New Orleans, Louisiana

Jim Taylor

Jim Taylor played with LSU in 1954 and from 1956 to 1957. During his time as a fullback with LSU, Taylor rushed for 1,314 yards and scored 20 rushing touchdowns. He was selected as an All-American player and earned All-SEC honors his senior year with LSU. In 1958, Taylor was drafted by the Green Bay Packers. He stayed with the Packers until he left for the New Orleans Saints in 1967. Taylor finished his 10-year NFL playing career with 8,597 yards and 83 rushing touchdowns. He was inducted into the Pro Football **Hall of Fame** in 1976.

Position: Fullback
Seasons: 1954, 1956–1957 (LSU Tigers), 1958–1966 (Green Bay Packers), 1967 (New Orleans Saints)
Born: September 20, 1935, Baton Rouge, Louisiana

Y.A. Tittle Jr.

Yelberton Abraham "Y.A." Tittle Jr. played football for LSU during World War II (1939–1945). During his freshman year, he set a school record with 238 passing yards in a single game. Tittle was drafted by the Detroit Lions in the 1948 NFL draft. However, he chose to play for the Baltimore Colts in the American Football League instead. The Colts failed as a team, and Tittle was drafted by the San Francisco 49ers in 1951. He became the first football player to appear on the cover of *Sports Illustrated*. Tittle was inducted into the Pro Football Hall of Fame in 1971.

Position: Quarterback
Seasons: 1944–1947 (LSU Tigers), 1948–1950 (Baltimore Colts), 1951–1960 (San Francisco 49ers), 1961–1964 (New York Giants)
Born: October 24, 1926, Marshall, Texas

All-Time Records

4,557

Career Rushing Yards

Kevin Faulk gained a total of 4,557 rushing yards from 1995 to 1998, an LSU career record.

31

Career Wins

With 31 career wins from 1986 to 1989, Tommy Hodson holds the LSU record for most wins by a starting quarterback.

53

Career Starts

Offensive tackle Ciron Black holds LSU's record for most career starts, with 53 games from 2006 to 2009.

61

Career Field Goals

From 1986 to 1989, kicker David Browndyke made 61 out of his 75 attempted field goals, an LSU record.

183

Career Receptions

Wendell Davis made a record 183 catches for the Tigers from 1984 to 1987.

Timeline

Throughout the team's history, the LSU Tigers have had many memorable events that have become defining moments for the team and its fans.

1893
The Tigers football team plays its first game on November 25.

1924
Tiger Stadium is completed.

1931
LSU begins the long tradition of playing night games. Some say it is to beat the heat and humidity of days in Louisiana, but fans say that night games are good luck for LSU.

1958
LSU's second undefeated team in school history beats Clemson in the Sugar Bowl to claim the national title.

1900 | 1920 | 1940 | 1960

In 1924, the Louisiana State University Tiger Marching Band opens the first home game of the season. The marching band opens home games with an intricate drum cadence followed by LSU's fight song.

1933
LSU joins the Southeastern Conference.

The Future

Since the 2000 season, LSU has made an impressive comeback. The Tigers have won two National Championships in the last decade and are considered one of the fiercest teams in the SEC. Their successful 2018 season hints at great things to come for the team under Head Coach Ed Orgeron.

2016

Ed Orgeron is hired as head coach. Orgeron leads the team into a successful era of LSU Football.

1995

Head Coach Gerry DiNardo petitions the NCAA to let LSU have its white home jerseys back. The NCAA agrees.

1980 — 2000 — 2020

2007

Head Coach Les Miles leads the team to its third National Championship.

In 2014, Tiger Stadium is expanded to hold a record number of fans. Its capacity reaches 102,321, almost 10 times more seats than when it originally opened.

1959

LSU player Billy Cannon is awarded the Heisman Memorial Trophy. He is the first and only LSU player to have been given the honor.

Write a Biography

Life Story

A person's life story can be the subject of a book. This kind of book is called a biography. Biographies often describe the lives of people who have achieved great success. These people may be alive today, or they may have lived many years ago. Reading a biography can help you learn more about a great person.

Get the Facts

Use this book, and research in the library and on the internet, to find out more about your favorite player. Learn as much about him as you can. What position does he play? What are his statistics in important categories? Has he set any records? Also, be sure to write down key events in the person's life. What was his childhood like? What has he accomplished off the field? Is there anything else that makes this person special or unusual?

Use the Concept Web

A concept web is a useful research tool. Read the questions in the concept web on the following page. Answer the questions in your notebook. Your answers will help you write a biography.

Concept Web

Write a Biography

Adulthood
- Where does this individual currently reside?
- Does he have a family?

Your Opinion
- What did you learn from the books you read in your research?
- Would you suggest these books to others?
- Was anything missing from these books?

Childhood
- Where and when was this person born?
- Describe his parents, siblings, and friends.
- Did he grow up in unusual circumstances?

Accomplishments off the Field
- What is this person's life's work?
- Has he received awards or recognition for accomplishments?
- How have this person's accomplishments served others?

Help and Obstacles
- Did this individual have a positive attitude?
- Did he receive help from others?
- Did this person have a mentor?
- Did this person face any hardships?
- If so, how were the hardships overcome?

Accomplishments on the Field
- What records does this person hold?
- What key games and plays have defined his career?
- What are his stats in categories important to his position?

Work and Preparation
- What was this person's education?
- What was his work experience?
- How does this person work?
- What is the process he uses?

Trivia Time

Take this quiz to test your knowledge of the LSU Tigers. The answers are printed upside down under each question.

1 Why did LSU stop bringing the live Mike the Tiger to games?

A. The sixth Mike refused to get into the cage that was wheeled into games.

2 How many Mike the Tigers have there been?

A. Seven

3 How many fans can Tiger Stadium hold?

A. More than 100,000

4 What is the record number of fans that Tiger Stadium has held?

A. 102,321

5 What are LSU's school colors?

A. Purple and gold

6 Who brought back the traditional white home jerseys?

A. Gerry DiNardo

7 Where is LSU located?

A. Baton Rouge, Louisiana, on the banks of the Mississippi River

8 How many rushing yards did Leonard Fournette III have during the 2015 season?

A. 1,953

9 What is Tiger Stadium's nickname?

A. Death Valley

10 Who opens home games for LSU?

A. The Louisiana State University Tiger Marching Band

Key Words

decorated: given an award for an outstanding accomplishment

drafted: chosen to play professionally in the National Football League during an annual event

habitat: the natural home environment of a living thing

Hall of Fame: a group of persons judged to be outstanding in a particular sport

matchups: contests between two athletes or sports teams

postseason: a sporting event that takes place after the end of the regular season

renovations: construction that works to improve or expand an older building

roster: a list of people who belong to a certain group or team

seismograph: an instrument that measures the force and length of earthquakes

stunts: daring and often difficult actions requiring skill to perform

Index

Log on to www.av2books.com

AV² by Weigl brings you media enhanced books that support active learning. Go to www.av2books.com, and enter the special code found on page 2 of this book. You will gain access to enriched and enhanced content that supplements and complements this book. Content includes video, audio, weblinks, quizzes, a slideshow, and activities.

AV² Online Navigation

AV² was built to bridge the gap between print and digital. We encourage you to tell us what you like and what you want to see in the future.

Sign up to be an AV² Ambassador at www.av2books.com/ambassador.

Due to the dynamic nature of the internet, some of the URLs and activities provided as part of AV² by Weigl may have changed or ceased to exist. AV² by Weigl accepts no responsibility for any such changes. All media enhanced books are regularly monitored to update addresses and sites in a timely manner. Contact AV² by Weigl at 1-866-649-3445 or av2books@weigl.com with any questions, comments, or feedback.